# My Body

Sue Barraclough

alphabet
soup

WINDMILL
BOOKS

Published in 2009 in the United States by Windmill Books, LLC
303 Park Avenue South, Suite #1280, New York, NY 10010-3657

U.S. publication copyright © Wayland Publishing 2009
First North American edition

Design and typography: Natascha Frensch
Read Regular (European Community Design Registration 2008)
Read Regular and Read Xheavy copyright © Natascha Frensch 2001-2007

Publisher Cataloging Data

Barraclough, Sue
    My body / Sue Barraclough.
        p.   cm.—(Me and my world)
    Includes index.
    Summary:  Simple text and photographs introduce parts of the body,
    including eyes, nose, mouth, ears, and arms.
    ISBN 978-1-60754-057-1 (library binding)
    ISBN 978-1-60754-062-5 (paperback)
    ISBN 978-1-60754-063-2 (6-pack)
1.  Body, Human—Juvenile literature   [1.  Body, Human   2.  Vocabulary]
I.  Title   II.  Series
    612—dc22

Manufactured in China

Photo Credits: Cover © Laureen Morgane/Corbis; p 1 Mike Powell/Taxi/Getty

2

# Contents

3

# body

I have a **body**.

arm

foot

A **body** has different parts.

hand

leg

5

# face

I have a **face**.

I can make funny **faces**.

# eyes

I have two **eyes**.

I use my **eyes** to see

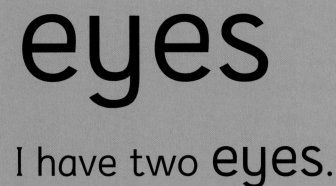

# nose

I have a **nose**.

We smell things with our **noses**.

# mouth

I have a **mouth**.

I use my mouth to speak.

# ears

I have two **ears**.

I hear with my ears.

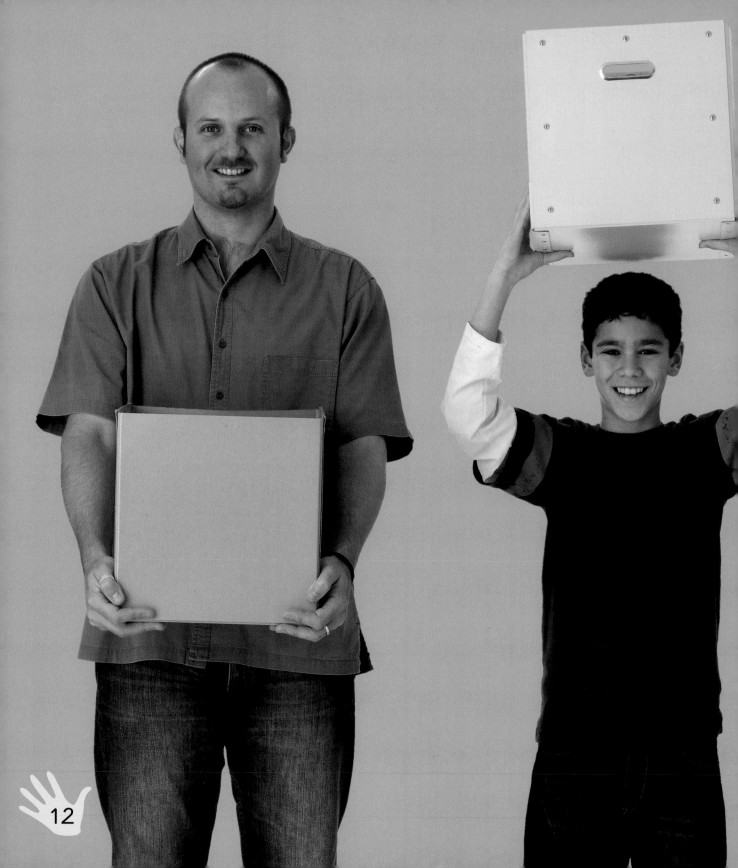

# arms

I have two **arms**.

We carry things with our **arms**.

# hands

I have two **hands.**

I can hold things in my **hand.**

15

# legs

I have two **legs**.

We use our legs for walking.

17

# feet

I have two **feet.**

I can walk with my **feet.**

# toes

I have **toes.**

20

We have ten ticklish **toes** each!

# Picture Quiz Game

Can you find these words in the book?

smell

hear

speak

see

What pages are they on?

# Index Quiz Game

The index is on page 24.
Use the index to help you
answer these questions.

1. Which page shows a funny face?
   What color is the boy's hair?

2. Which pages show six legs?
   How many boots can you count?

3. Which page shows smelly flowers?
   What color are the flowers?

4. Which pages show ticklish toes?
   How many big toes can you count?

# Index and Web Sites

## Answers
**Picture Quiz Game:** Smell is on page 9, Hear is on page 11, Speak is on page 10, See is on page 8.
**Index Quiz Game:** 1. page 7, black; 2. pages 16-17, four; 3. page 9, yellow; 4. pages 20-21, six.

### Web Sites
To ensure the currency and safety of recommended Internet links, Windmill maintains and updates an online list of sites related to the subject of this book. To access this list of Web sites, please go to www.windmillbooks.com/weblinks and select this book's title.

For more great fiction and nonfiction, go to windmillbooks.com.